Mr. WILLIAM
SHAKESPEARES

COMEDIES,
HISTORIES, &
TRAGEDIES.

Publiſhed according to the True Originall Copies.

Martin Droeſhout ſculpſit London

LONDON
Printed by Iſaac Iaggard, and Ed. Blount. 1623.

THE
TEMPEST.

Actus primus, Scena prima.

A tempestuous noise of Thunder and Lightning heard :. Enter a Ship-master, and a Botefwaine.

Master.

BOte-fwaine.

Botef. Heere Mafter : What cheere ?

Maft. Good :-Speake to th'Mariners : fall too't, yarely, or we run our felues a ground, beftirre, beftirre. *Exit.*

Enter Mariners.

Botef. Heigh my hearts, cheerely, cheerely my harts : yare, yare : Take in the toppe-fale : Tend to th'Mafters whiftle : Blow till thou burft thy winde , if roome e nough.

Enter Alonfo, Sebaftian, Anthonio, Ferdinando, Gonzalo, and others.

Alon. Good Botefwaine haue care : where's the Mafter ? Play the men.

Botef. I pray now keepe below.

Anth. Where is the Mafter, Bofon ?

Botef. Do you not heare him ? you marre our labour, Keepe your Cabines : you do afsift the ftorme.

Gonz. Nay, good be patient.

Botef. When the Sea is: hence, what cares thefe roa-rers for the name of King ? to Cabine; filence : trouble vs not.

Gon. Good, yet remember whom thou haft aboord.

Botef. None that I more loue then my felfe. You are a Counfellor, if you can command thefe Elements to fi-lence, and worke the peace of the prefent, wee will not hand a rope more, vfe your authoritie : If you cannot, giue thankes you haue liu'd fo long, and make your felfe readie in your Cabine for the mifchance of the houre, if it fo hap. Cheerely good hearts : out of our way I fay. *Exit.*

Gon. I haue great comfort from this fellow : methinks he hath no drowning marke vpon him, his complexion is perfect Gallowes : ftand faft good Fate to his han-ging, make the rope of his deftiny our cable, for our owne doth little aduantage : If he be not borne to bee hang'd, our cafe is miferable. *Exit.*

Enter Botefwaine.

Botef. Downe with the top-Maft : yare, lower, lower, bring her to Try with Maine-courfe. A plague ——

A cry within. Enter Sebaftian, Anthonio & Gonzalo.

vpon this howling : they are lowder then the weather, or our office : yet againe ? What do you heere ? Shal we giue ore and drowne, haue you a minde to finke ?

Sebaf. A poxe o'your throat, you bawling, blafphe-mous incharitable Dog.

Botef. Worke you then.

Anth. Hang cur, hang, you whorefon infolent Noyfe-maker, we are leffe afraid to be drownde, then thou art.

Gonz. I'le warrant him for drowning , though the Ship were no ftronger then a Nutt-fhell, and as leaky as an vnftanched wench.

Botef. Lay her a hold, a hold , fet her two courfes off to Sea againe, lay her off.

Enter Mariners wet.

Mari. All loft, to prayers, to prayers, all loft.

Botef. What muft our mouths be cold ?

Gonz. The King, and Prince, at prayers, let's afsift them, for our cafe is as theirs.

Sebaf. I'am out of patience.

An. We are meerly cheated of our liues by drunkards, This wide-chopt-rafcall, would thou mightft lye drow-ning the wafhing of ten Tides.

Gonz. Hee'l be hang'd yet, Though euery drop of water fweare againft it, And gape at widft to glut him. *A confufed noyfe within.* Mercy on vs.

We fplit, we fplit , Farewell my wife and children, Farewell brother : we fplit, we fplit, we fplit.

Anth. Let's all finke with' King

Seb. Let's take leaue of him. *Exit.*

Gonz. Now would I giue a thoufand furlongs of Sea, for an Acre of barren ground : Long heath , Browne firrs, any thing; the wills aboue be done, but I would faine dye a dry death. *Exit.*

Scena Secunda.

Enter Profpero and Miranda.

Mira. If by your Art (my deereft father) you haue Put the wild waters in this Rore; alay them : The skye it feemes would powre down ftinking pitch, But that the Sea, mounting to th' welkins cheeke, Dafhes the fire out. Oh ! I haue fuffered With thofe that I faw fuffer : A braue veffell

A   (Who

a workshop approach to

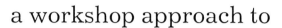

MPEST

Exmouth

m Five

ıder

ı Watson

y John Hughes

THE SHAKESPEARE WORKSHOP SERIES
General Editor: Peter Jones

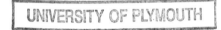

St Clair Press

The Tempest, **Full Fathom Five** is published by St Clair Press
an imprint of PHOENIX EDUCATION PTY LTD

Sydney
PO Box 3141, Putney 2112
Tel: (02) 9809 3579 Fax: (02) 9808 1430

Melbourne
PO Box 197, Albert Park 3206
Tel: (03) 9699 8377 Fax: (03) 9699 9242

Email: service@phoenixeduc.com
Website: www.phoenixeduc.com

Printing:
Printed in Australia by Five Senses Education, Seven Hills

Contents

Preface to the Revised Edition

Recent scholarship, especially the work of the new historicists, has prompted some revision of the late Brenda Pinder's valuable teaching aid. In particular a new activity (No.12) invites students to look at the play through the lens of post-colonialism. Another new activity (No.21) involves a consideration of the BBC television version of the play, and a final activity draws attention to some significant stage productions.

Use has also been made of a recent edition of the play in the Cambridge University Press series, *Shakespeare in Production*. This volume, edited by Christine Dymkowski, (2000) offers line-by-line accounts of how actors and directors over the last four hundred years have interpreted the play, and thus offers a wealth of material for class discussion of a play that permits a remarkable range of interpretations. A copy of this edition would prove a valuable addition to the teaching materials presented in *Full Fathom Five*.

Alternative Viewpoint: Caliban

– Evidence –

EXAMPLE 1

Caliban: *This island's mine, by Sycorax my mother,*
           Which thou tak'st from me. When thou cam'st first,
           Thou strok'st me, and made much of me; wouldst give me
           Water with berries in 't; and teach me how
           To name the bigger light, and how the less,
           That burn by day and night: and then I lov'd thee,
           And show'd thee all the qualities o' th' isle,
           The fresh springs, brine-pits, barren place and fertile:
           Curs'd be I that did so! All the charms
           Of Sycorax, toads, beetles, bats, light on you!
           For I am all the subjects that you have,
           Which first was mine own King: and here you sty me
           In this hard rock, whiles you do keep from me
           The rest o' th' island.

                                                                          (I ii 333-346)

EXAMPLE 2

Caliban: *Be not afeard; the isle is full of noises,*
           Sounds and sweet airs, that give delight, and hurt not.
           Sometimes a thousand twangling instruments
           Will hum about mine ears; and sometime voices,
           That, if I then had wak'd after long sleep,
           Will make me sleep again: and then, in dreaming,
           The clouds methought would open, and show riches
           Ready to drop upon me; that, when I wak'd,
           I cried to dream again.

                                                                          (III ii 133-141)

– Activity –

You may feel there is some justice in Caliban's claim to own the island and in his bitterness against Prospero. Remind yourself how Caliban came to the island (I ii 269-286). From his point of view Prospero must seem a usurper, and unjust in his treatment of Caliban. (Though we hear from Prospero the reasons for this.)

Skim through the text to find scenes in which Caliban appears. How much of the events on the island might he be aware of? (Storm? Ferdinand?) Make notes on how he might see these things.

Now use your notes to write Caliban's account, in the form of a diary or interior monologue, of all he has seen and heard during the course of the play (and some time before). Try to interpret events the way he would and to capture his characteristic language. Remember he is not unaware of the beauties and natural wealth of the island. (III ii 133-141 and II ii 160-172.)

– Follow Up –

Write a short paragraph by each of the following *about* Caliban:
• Prospero
• Miranda
• Stephano
• Trinculo

In what important point(s) would each of these views of Caliban differ from Caliban's own understanding or point of view?

The Story So Far

– Evidence –

The play begins as Prospero's plans for revenge on Alonso and his brother are coming to fruition; he has them on his island, driven there by his magical storm, and held in his power by Ariel. The plot of the play is grounded in events that precede it, and early scenes involve a lot of background storytelling.

- Remind yourself of the account Prospero gives Miranda of how they came to be there. (I ii 33 onwards)

- Look at his reminders to Ariel of how he rescued Ariel from the cloven pine (270-293) and to Caliban, about how his trust was betrayed. (I ii 332-367)

– Activity –

Imagine you are writing a story for young children – say eight to ten year-olds – and describe the magical events that have happened before the play in a language and style they would readily understand. You may also include the Miranda story, and finish by telling them that Prospero now has all his enemies in his power.

You may wish to illustrate your story with your own drawings or a collage of fragments cut from magazines.

The exercise will help to clarify your own understanding of the plot and the workings of Prospero's magic which prepare us for his later schemes.

– Follow Up –

Collect the stories together and offer them to a local primary school. Perhaps their teacher would ask the children to write their predictions of what they think will happen on the island and let you see their forecasts.

Or you could act out the story for a young audience, perhaps with storyteller and mime.

On And Off

– Evidence –

The chart below lists main characters and scenes:

	i	ii	i	ii	i	ii	iii	Act IV	Act V
Prospero									
Miranda									
Ferdinand									
Ariel									
Caliban									
Alonso									
Gonzalo									
Antonio									
Sebastian									
Trinculo									
Stephano									
Master & Crew									
Goddesses									
	Act I		Act II		Act III				

– Activity –

This exercise is to help you sort out various threads of the plot. On the chart on the previous page mark entrances and exits of the major characters. You could subdivide some of the very long scenes by page numbers to make arrivals and departures clearer.

You can also add more detail to this simple chart by using different colours to represent various threads of the plot. Any scene that develops, say, the Miranda-Ferdinand story and the Prospero-Caliban one would have the two different colours marked on it. Try to develop the idea with your own suggestions to make the storylines clearer: it is far easier to remember things you have recorded in visual form.

– Follow Up –

Invent your own version of Prospero's island and make a map of it, marking the important locations like Prospero's cell, where Ferdinand lands, etc, and plot onto it the routes taken by the various groups of characters until they all meet at the end.

Relationships:
Visual Presentation

– Evidence –

Look up these aspects of Prospero's relationships with others in the play.

- To Miranda, Prospero describes his brother as "false" (I ii 77, 92), yet in the final scene (V i 78-9) he forgives him.

- He tells Miranda that Ferdinand is a "traitor" (I ii 463), yet the audience knows by his asides that this is pretence.

- He abuses Caliban (I ii) yet acknowledges him as his own. (V i 275-6)

These are just a few of the conflicting pieces of evidence to be considered in looking at his relationships. They suggest that Prospero is a complex character and that his feelings towards others are far from simple.

– Activity –

Look at the spider charts *on the next page*, which are intended to clarify your interpretations of Prospero's underlying feelings about the characters round the outside. On the *first* chart write a short quotation along the arrow to sum up what you decide is Prospero's view of each. (They may or may not be lines spoken by Prospero.)

On the *second* chart, which reverses the direction of the arrows, find quotations to indicate the feelings of each of the characters about **Prospero.**

– Follow Up –

Choose any other character from the play and repeat the exercise. (You will find it is easier to remember things if you have put them down in a visual, diagrammatic form.

You may be able to devise other ways of presenting your ideas, with quotations to illustrate them, in visual form. Share any ideas you have with the rest of the class.

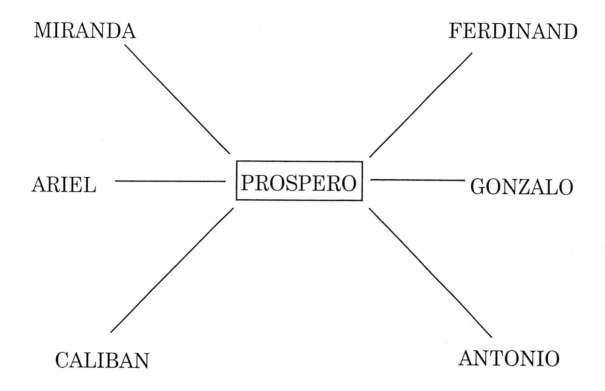

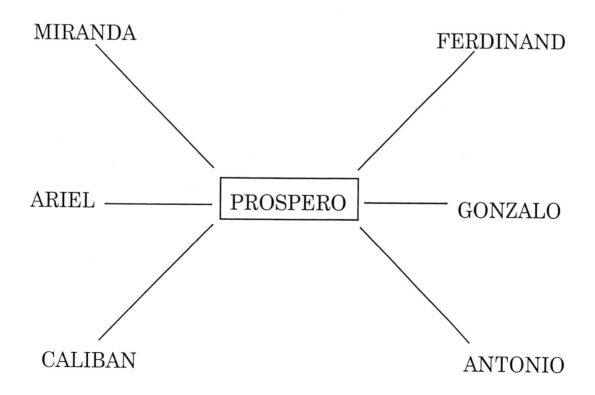

The Masque in Freeze Frames

– Evidence –

Cer: *Tell me, heavenly bow,*
If Venus or her son, as thou dost know,
Do now attend the queen? Since they did plot
The means that dusky Dis my daughter got,
Her and her blind boy's scandal'd company
I have forsworn.

Iris.   *Of her society*
Be not afraid: I met her deity
Cutting the clouds towards Paphos, and her son
Dove-drawn with her. Here thought they to have done
Wove wanton charm upon this man and maid,
Whose vows are, that no bed-right shall be paid
Till Hymen's torch be lighted: but in vain;
Mars's hot minion is return'd again;
Her waspish-headed son has broke his arrows,
Swears he will shoot no more, but play with sparrows,
And be a boy right out.

Cer.   *Highest queen of State,*
Great Juno comes; I know her by her gait.

Juno.   *How does my bounteous sister? Go with me*
To bless this twain, that they may prosperous be,
And honour'd in their issue.   (They sing:)

Juno.   *Honour, riches, marriage-blessing,*
Long continuance, and increasing,
Hourly joys be still upon you!
Juno sings her blessings on you.

Cer.   *Earth's increase, foison plenty,*
Barns and garners never empty;
Vines with clust'ring bunches growing;
Plants with goodly burthen bowing;
Spring come to you at the farthest
In the very end of harvest!
Scarcity and Want shall shun you;
Ceres' blessing so is on you.

The Masque is often omitted from modern productions yet the images and symbols of these lines are central to the play. Venus and her son Cupid are put to flight and chastity promises the rewards of plenty and fruitfulness. Prospero has already warned Ferdinand that if he should "break her virgin knot" before the ceremonies of marriage then discord and "loathly weeds" (IV i 13-23) will follow. Gonzalo has seen the island as "lush and lusty" (II i 51) and Adrian finds that the air "breathes upon us here most sweetly" (45), while those who are deaf to the music of the island (see activity called *Music and Songs*) are also blind to its fertility and beauty. Sebastian and Antonio find it "as 'twere perfum'd by a fen" (47) and without means to sustain life; they ridicule Gonzalo's vision of a pastoral idyll. (139-179) Reactions to the beauty of the island by each character may point to certain sensibilities and sympathetic (or unsympathetic) states of mind. (Exploration of different states of mind is an important aspect of the play.)

– Activity –

Divide into threes or fours and read aloud the whole of the Masque, noticing the formality of the language and the stylised presentation of the goddesses. Now devise a series of freeze frames – about five tableaux – to represent the content of the speeches. Realism is not required so concentrate on symbolism to create a series of images with your bodies. Present these, accompanied by words, to the rest of the class.

– Follow Up –

Investigate the traditions of the masque form with the help of an encyclopedia or reference book on the theatre.

Then compare the language Shakespeare uses here (which is a kind of serious parody of the traditional style of the masque) with that of the rest of the play. Notice the rhyming couplets, images of idealised pastoral scene, lack of colloquial directness, etc, and find contrasting examples from the rest of the play.

Ten Years On

– Evidence –

The following lines are all from the last scene: (V i)

Prospero: *I'll break my staff*
Bury it certain fadoms in th' earth
And deeper than did ever plummet sound,
I'll drown my book.   (54-57)

Prosero: *But you, my brace of lords, were I so minded,*
I here could pluck his highness' frown upon you,
And justify you traitors: at this time
I will tell no tales.   (126-129)

Gonzalo: *Was Milan thrust from Milan, that his issue*
Should become kings of Naples?   (205-206)

Prospero: *This thing of darkness I*
Acknowledge mine.   (275-276)

Prospero: *And thence retire me to my Milan, where*
Every third thought shall be my grave.   (310-311)

Look up the context of these lines. What do they suggest might follow, after the end of the play?

• Prospero intends to rule Milan without his magic. Will this prove difficult?

• What are the prospects for Ferdinand and Miranda's married happiness?

• Prospero accepts responsibility for Caliban. Will he take him to Milan? If so, what will life be like for him there?

• Prospero decides not to tell Alonso about Sebastian and Antonio's treachery. Do they show any signs of repentance?

– Activity –

Working in pairs, imagine all the characters after ten more years and discuss what you think might be happening to them. Will Prospero make the same mistakes as last time? Will there be more trouble from Antonio?

How will Sebastian react to the rediscovery of Ferdinand, Alonso's heir? What will life be like for Caliban in the new Milan? Prepare notes on these and any other points that interest you for a class discussion.

– Follow Up –

- Improvise, in groups, on life in Milan and Naples ten years on. Remember that the forecast you make is not directly relevant to your study of the play – only in the light it sheds on character and theme in the play itself.

- Write an essay on the theme of reconciliation and forgiveness in the play.

Order and Disorder

– Evidence –

The usurping of Prospero's rule of Milan by his brother, and Alonso, is not the only example of natural order overthrown in the play. Consider the following examples:

- The storm: the overthrow of nature's order

- Antonio and Sebastian's plot to murder Alonso and take over Naples (II i 201-90)

- The plot of Caliban, Stephano and Trinculo to overthrow Prospero's rule of the island (III ii 85-93) which is a kind of parody of the initiating action all those years ago in Milan

To the Elizabethans, the bond between subject and ruler would have seemed as natural as that between brothers; both of these loyalties are cast aside by those who rebel in the play. But was Prospero himself guilty in any way? Did his neglect of his duties as a ruler in order to pursue his studies amount to an overthrow of the natural order? Or is this taking the idea too far?

– Activity –

Antonio, Sebastian, Alonso and Caliban are all to be put on trial for their rebellions, and they, in turn, will accuse Prospero.

Divide into five groups – one to put Prospero's view and one to plead mitigating circumstances in the case of each of the others. You will need to collect as much evidence from the actual lines of the play as you can, to argue your particular case.

When you have prepared the material, hold a public investigation. The Prospero group accuses each of the others in turn; they defend themselves as well as they can and point out Prospero's own faults in their case.

Try to devise a way in which the proceedings can be brought to a satisfactory conclusion – perhaps with Prospero's lines of forgiveness for each of them.

– Follow Up –

The theme of nature and of what constitutes natural behaviour is worth exploring. Skim the text for examples of the use of the word 'natural' (you may have done this in the activity called *Patterns of Imagery*) and make a list of all the natural bonds you can find between characters. Then look closely at the Masque (see also the activity on this) and especially at Ceres, Goddess of Nature and Fertility. Check on the opposing views of the natural surroundings of the island offered by Gonzalo, Sebastian and Antonio in II i, and on the warnings of Prospero to Ferdinand in IV i 13-23.

Using all these, prepare notes on the theme of nature and fertility in the play and discuss your points with a partner. You could then develop your ideas in a longer piece of writing on this theme.

Film Adaptation

– Evidence –

ENTER Prospero and Miranda.

Miranda: *If by your Art, my dearest father, you have*
Put the wild waters in this roar, allay them.
The sky, it seems, would pour down stinking pitch,
But that the sea, mounting to th' welkin's cheek,
Dashes the fire out. O, I have suffered
With those that I saw suffer! a brave vessel,
(Who had, no doubt, some noble creature in her,)
Dash'd all to pieces. O, the cry did knock
Against my very heart! Poor souls, they perish'd!
Had I been any god of power, I would
Have sunk the sea within the earth, or ere
It should the good ship so have swallow'd, and
The fraughting souls within her.

Prospero: *Be collected:*
No more amazement: tell your piteous heart
There's no harm done.

Miranda: *O, woe the day!*

Prospero: *No harm.*
I have done nothing but in care of thee,
Of thee, my dear one; thee, my daughter, who
Art ignorant of what thou art; nought knowing
Of whence I am, nor that I am more better
Than Prospero, master of a full poor cell,
And thy no greater father.

Miranda: *More to know*
Did never meddle with my thoughts.

Prospero: *Tis time*
I should inform thee farther. Lend thy hand,
And pluck my magic garment from me. — So:

                                                        [Lays
down his mantle]
Lie there, my Art. Wipe thou thine eyes; have comfort.
The direful spectacle of the wrack, which touch'd
The very virtue of compassion in thee,
I have with such provision in mine Art
So safety ordered, that there is no soul —
No, not so much perdition as an hair
Betid to any creature in the vessel
Which thou heard'st cry, which thou saw'st sink.
        Sit down;
For thou must now know farther.

These are the opening speeches of I ii, the first scene that takes place on the island, the first scene being the storm at sea.

– Activity –

As with the activity called *Prompt Copy*, the purpose of this activity is to create drama out of a printed script, but this time in terms of film rather than theatre. Concentrating on the opening conversation between Prospero and Miranda, think what images you would want to show your audience before the actors begin to speak. Would you want a general view of the island from above? Would you then zoom in to Prospero's cell? Or are there other images you would want to project even before this? – say, the sea itself, still wild after the storm, as Miranda's first words suggest?

Make a list of camera shots (there's no need to worry about technical words, though `closeup' and 'panorama' can be useful), which would precede and accompany these first few speeches. Remember that in a film the director chooses what the audience will see, and concentrate on, far more specifically than the theatre producer.

Decide whose face we should look at while Prospero and Miranda speak: it does not, of course, have to be the speaker. You can also direct our eyes towards scenes and objects – the sea, Prospero's cloak, the books in his cell, etc.

Perhaps the best way to present your work is to paste the script of the section you are doing on the left of a sheet of paper and write camera shots next to it on the right.

Share ideas with the rest of the class by displaying them or handing them round and talking about them.

– Follow Up –

Some effective writing can come out of this process too. Remove from your list all references to the camera, leaving just a list of images, and write them underneath one another, one image to a line. The result can be a surprisingly vivid poem. Try it with your list, revising and adding to your first draft until you are satisfied with it. Then make a copy for display, to share your response with others.

Prospero's Magic

– Evidence –

Working in pairs, look up the following references and discuss what they show you about the purpose and results of Prospero's magic.

1. The Storm – how do we learn it is the result of his magic? (Miranda I ii 1-2 and Ariel, 198-237)

2. Ariel (instructed by Prospero I ii 319) leads Ferdinand with his song to meet Miranda (I ii 377). How do we know Ferdinand's and Miranda's reactions (496-7) are what Prospero intended?

3. Ariel's music puts to sleep all of Alonso's party except Sebastian and Antonio (II i 185) and wakes them to avert danger (295). What do you think was Prospero's purpose in putting them to sleep in the first place?

4. Prospero watches Ferdinand and Miranda while invisible. (III i 15 onwards) What can we deduce from his asides?

5. Ariel's interventions in the conversations between Caliban, Stephano and Trinculo cause strife between them. (III ii 40 onwards) Is this just mischief or averting danger again?

6. Prospero presents a banquet which is snatched away before it can be eaten. (III iii 18 and 52) What is Prospero's intention in this trick? How is it symbolic of earlier behaviour? Look closely at Ariel's Harpy speech: what is the effect on the guilty?

7. Notice how Prospero's sudden recollection of the Caliban plot breaks up the magic of the Masque. (See activity called *The Masque in Freeze Frames*.)

8. What aspects of Ariel's punishment of the Caliban party (IV i 171 and 254) and the temptation of them with "glistering apparel" (193) are paralleled elsewhere in the story?

9. Prospero's renunciation of his magic (V i 50-7) after a summary of what his powers have achieved: who shows him that the only truly human course is to forgive his enemies?

– Activity –

In pairs, compose a dialogue between Prospero and Ariel at the final moment of the play. Ariel questions Prospero about his magic, how he found such power, what he was trying to achieve by it, etc, and Prospero answers him before finally saying goodbye.

Each pair performs their dialogue to another pair, comparing interpretations.

– Follow Up –

Ariel and Caliban are sometimes thought of as the two sides of Prospero's nature – Caliban the animal side, Ariel the learning and power of the mind. Can you find any supporting evidence for this theory? Notice that Prospero does not reject Caliban at the end of the play:

> *"this thing of darkness I*
> *Acknowledge mine.' (V i 275-6)*

Ariel and Caliban never speak to each other in the play, though Caliban is aware of Ariel's music. (III ii 133) Why should this be?

You might like to write on the relationship of Ariel and Prospero in the play. Look at the way they address one another as well as at the examples of magic above.

You might also consider writing about how magic creates both punishment and reconciliation in *The Tempest*.

Music and Songs

– Evidence –

ARIEL['s] song.
Come unto these yellow sands,
 And then take hands:
Courtsied when you have and kiss'd
 The wild waves whist:
Foot it featly here and there,
 And sweet sprites bear
The burthen. Hark, hark.

Burthen dispersedly. *Bow-wow.*

The watch dogs bark:

[Burthen dispersedly.] *Bow-wow.*

Hark, hark! I hear
The strain of strutting chanticleer

Cry [Burthen dispersedly.] *Cock a didle dow.*

(I ii 377-389)

ARIEL['s] song.
Full fadom five thy father lies;
 Of his bones are coral made;
Those are pearls that were his eyes:
 Nothing of him that doth fade,
But doth suffer a sea-change
 Into something rich and strange.
Sea-nymphs hourly ring his knell:

Burthen: *Ding-dong.*

Hark! now I hear them, — Ding-dong, bell.

(I ii 399-407)

Ferdinand, in line 394, bears witness to the magical powers of Ariel's music, which seems to pacify both the waves and his own troubled spirits.

In the image of the bones of his father transformed by a "sea-change" into "something rich and strange" there is perhaps an allegory of the whole play; some of those affected by Prospero's magic, like Alonso, are indeed transformed and reborn. T S Eliot, in *The Waste Land*, uses these very lines to set against his allegorical desert landscape of modern life where he finds little evidence of "sea-change". So Ariel's songs seem more than decorative: they present us with echoes of the play's themes and images.

– Activity –

Take a close look at all the songs and references to music listed below:

1. Music is used to put Alonso and others to sleep and to alert them to danger. (II i 179-185 and 295-300) Why do Antonio and Sebastian only speak of a "hollow burst of bellowing"? (306) Were they just covering up?

2. Stephano's and Caliban's drunken ditties. (II ii 43-55 and 178-185)

3. Panic is created in Stephano and Trinculo by Ariel's intervention. (III ii 119-121) Caliban is unafraid and sees the island's music as beneficial (132-141).

4. The Banquet placed before Alonso's party is accompanied by "solemn and strange music". (III iii 18 and 82)

5. "Soft music" accompanies the words of the goddesses in the Masque (IV i) and the whole culminates in a "graceful dance" in which harmonious movement and music combine. When Prospero remembers the Caliban conspiracy, music turns to "a strange hollow and confused noise". (138)

6. In the last scene, Prospero uses "heavenly music" (52) to calm the anguish of his captives. As they are frozen under his charm, Ariel sings a song full of natural images. (88, 94)

Discuss all these examples with a partner.

*   What links can you find between music and magic?

*   Who hears and who is deaf to the music of the play? Why?

*   Is music linked with harmony in behaviour?

– Follow Up –

Look up references to *dance* in the play, and discuss how these are related to the music.

Patterns of Imagery

– Evidence –

When we look closely at most of Shakespeare's plays, we can find groups of recurring images – as though he were making connections and underlying threads as he was writing. Each time an image recurs, it comes to us with the cumulative force of the previous occasions, and repeated words and ideas gradually build a network of associations.

Look up the following examples – all from one scene (I ii) – and a few of their connections later in the play.

1.   *he was*
   The ivy which had hid my princely trunk,
   And suck'd my verdure out on't. (85-87)

   (*weeds so loathly*, IV i 21, picks up a similar idea)

2. *To have no screen between this part he play'd*
   And him he play'd it for, he needs will be
   Absolute Milan. (107-109)

   (compare with Prospero's "revels" speech in IV i 145-163)

3. *On their sustaining garments, not a blemish.* (218)
   (compare with Gonzalo's comments, II i 59-62)

4. *Jove's lightnings* and *the mighty Neptune* (201, 205)

   (compare with the Masque's goddesses)

5. *a freckled whelp, hag-born; thou tortoise* (283, 318) and *here you sty me in this hard rock* (344-345) are recalled when we realise Trinculo sees Caliban as a monster in II ii 25 onwards.

6. *pearls that were his eyes* (401) and *sea-change* (403) link with
   And deeper than did ever plummet sound
   I'll drown my book. (V i 56-57)

These are only a few of the possible verbal connections to be found with I ii.

– Activity –

Divide into four groups, each taking one of the remaining acts (ie, II-V). Look through it carefully and collect any striking images and echoes you can find, listing them under the following headings:

a) the natural world;

b) the sea/storm;

c) monsters and animals;

d) gods and goddesses;

e) sky and stars;

f) clothes;

g) acting and pretence;

h) any other effective images which are not included in the list.

Display your examples from each act under these headings and discuss them as a class.

– Follow Up –

Another striking feature of the language of *The Tempest* is the number of compound words – like "man-monster", "sea-change", "pinch-spotted", "inch-meal", etc.

Working in the same groups, find examples from your act and share them with other groups.

Individual work: Choose one or two of these compound expressions and explore their associations on the lines of the example below.

Add any others which occur to you on this diagram before you do the same with your chosen example. Then compare notes with a partner and discuss your word associations.

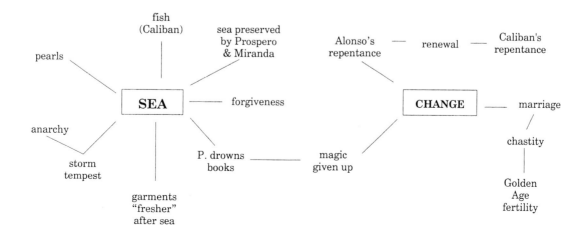

An Examination
of Colonialism

(Note to the teacher: The Open University, in conjunction with the BBC, has produced a video which looks at aspects of two plays, *Measure for Measure* and *The Tempest*. The section on *The Tempest* examines themes of colonialism, both Elizabethan and current, with reference to the play, and includes excerpts both from the BBC version [see Activity 21] and from a reworking of play by the West Indian/French dramatist Césaire, *Une Tempête*. In Australia, the video is available through Educational Media Australia, 214 Park St, South Melbourne 3205.)

– Evidence –

Unlike most of Shakespeare's plays, *The Tempest* is not based on some pre-existing story, but he was clearly making use of two important sources:

1. The voyages of colonists to Virginia, and in particular a storm off the Bermudas in 1609 which nearly wrecked the flagship *Sea Adventure*. The crew managed to land on one of the islands, and repair the ship, and several accounts of their experience were published.

2. Montaigne's *Of Cannibals*, which was translated into English in 1603. This book raised questions about the ethics of colonisation and idealised the 'cannibals'. Gonzalo's speech on the ideal commonwealth is a reworking of part of Montaigne's essay.

– Activity –

In your group, gather evidence from the play that would support a production emphasising the ethical questions raised by colonisation. For example, in the second scene Caliban, who in the cast list of the First Folio is described as "a salvage [savage] and deformed slave", says:

> *This island's mine, by Sycorax my mother,*
> *Which thou tak'st from me...*

What does the text actually tell us about the events which occurred when Prospero first reached the island?

Look carefully at Gonzalo's speech (Act II, sc.i) about his ideal commonwealth. Can you find any contradictions in it? How does it compare with the actual situation on Prospero's island?

Look carefully at the scene between Caliban and Stefano (II.ii). What does it tell us about Caliban's attitude to Europeans? What assumptions can we draw from the way he regards Stephano?

In the bowdlerised editions of *The Tempest* that were common in British and Australian schools until the 1950s, all reference to Caliban's attempted rape of Miranda was omitted. How would this omission affect one's view of the play?

In your group, imagine that you want to create sympathy for Caliban. What aspects of Prospero's character would you emphasise? What would you emphasise about Caliban?

"Caliban is an instructor in the arts of survival. He has lived alone on the island without any assistance from Prospero. Prospero, on the other hand, cannot survive without the assistance of Caliban."(Jonathan Bate, *The Genius of Shakespeare*, p245) How does Prospero win his help?

One of the ways in which an actor (or director) can colour the audience's attitude to a character is through the character's physical appearance. As Harold Bloom, in his recent book, *Shakespeare: the Invention of the Human*, has noted, in various productions Caliban has appeared as half-amphibian, an ape man, a Neanderthal, as well as the archetypal noble savage. Frequently black actors are cast in the role. In one strange production, Caliban was a tortoise-like creature who could be rendered powerless by being turned on his back. But what does the text really say about him? Bloom seems to accept that Caliban is half-amphibian, but, as David Suchet, a distinguished performer in the role, has pointed out, that interpretation, based on Trinculo's first speech (II.ii), refers to Caliban's smell, not his appearance:

A fish, he smells like a fish...a strange fish...his fins like arms

Not 'his arms like fins', but 'his fins like arms'.

In your group, note down all the references to Caliban's appearance, and then decide how he should appear on stage. (David Suchet's account of his investigations, and a photograph of him in the role appear in *Players of Shakespeare 1* ed. Philip Brockbank.)

In Peter Hall's 1974 production, Dennis Quilley's make-up as Caliban "was bisected: one half of his face presented the ugly deformed monster, the other an image of the noble savage. This meant that, in visual terms, by turning his profile to the audience he could change his appearance in a moment". (David Hirst, *The Tempest: Text and Performance*, p48) This ingenious solution to the problem of Caliban's appearance could, of course, only work in a particular kind of theatre.

Active Soliloquy

– Evidence –

Ye elves of hills, brooks, standing lakes, and groves;
And ye that on the sands with printless foot
Do chase the ebbing Neptune, and do fly him
When he comes back; you demi-puppets that
By moonshine do the green sour ringlets make,
Whereof the ewe not bites; and you whose pastime
Is to make midnight mushrooms, that rejoice
To hear the solemn curfew; by whose aid –
Weak masters though ye be – I have bedimm'd
The noontide sun, call'd forth the mutinous winds,
And 'twixt the green sea and the azur'd vault
Set roaring war: to the dread rattling thunder
Have I given fire, and rifted Jove's stout oak
With his own bolt; the strong-bas'd promontory
Have I made shake, and by the spurs pluck'd up
The pine and cedar: graves at my command
Have wak'd their sleepers, op'd, and let 'em forth
By my so potent Art. But this rough magic
I here abjure; and, when I have requir'd
Some heavenly music, – which even now I do, –
To work mine end upon their senses, that
This airy charm is for, I'll break my staff,
Bury it certain fadoms in the earth,
And deeper than did ever plummet sound
I'll drown my book.
    (V i 33-57)

– Activity –

This soliloquy of Prospero's, in which he calls up all the spirits of his magic art and gives them freedom is one of the most magnificent in the play. Read it to yourself and listen in your head to the sound and rhythms.

Now divide into groups of about six and devise a way of presenting the speech as a dramatic activity in itself. Do not try to be Prospero; divide the lines between you and become his thoughts. Some lines may be spoken in chorus, some by individual voices, and you can add movements or freeze frames to bring out the drama of the words. Place the actors in various parts of the room, perhaps, or use members of the group to represent the different creatures conjured up by Prospero. Use your imaginations and be as unrealistic as you like.

– Follow Up –

Use the same technique to present any other speech you choose, such as "Our revels now are ended" (IV i 48-58) or "You are three men of sin" (III iii 53-82).

Prompt Copy

– Evidence –

Prospero: *A solemn air, and the best comforter*
To an unsettled fancy, cure thy brains,
Now useless, boil'd within thy skull! There stand,
For you are spell-stopp'd.
Holy Gonzalo, honourable man,
Mine eyes, ev'n sociable to the show of thine,
Fall fellowly drops. The charm dissolves apace;
And as the morning steals upon the night,
Melting the darkness, so their rising senses
Begin to chase the ignorant fumes that mantle
Their clearer reason. O good Gonzalo,
My true preserver, and a loyal sir
To him thou follow'st! I will pay thy graces
Home both in word and deed. Most cruelly
Didst thou, Alonso, use me and my daughter:
Thy brother was a furtherer in the act.
Thou art pinch's for't now, Sebastian. Flesh and blood,
You, brother mine, that entertain'd ambition,
Expell'd remorse and nature; whom, with Sebastian, –
Whose inward pinches therefor are most strong, –
Would here have kill'd your King; I do forgive thee,
Unnatural though thou art. Their understanding
Begins to swell; and the approaching tide
Will shortly fill the reasonable shore,
That now lies foul and muddy. Not one of them
That yet looks on me, or would know me: Ariel,
Fetch me the hat and rapier in my cell:
I will discase me, and myself present
As I was sometime Milan: quickly, spirit;
Thou shalt ere long be free.

Ariel sings and helps to attire him.

Where the bee sucks, there suck I:
In a cowslip's bell I lie;
There I couch when owls do cry.
On the bat's back I do fly
After summer merrily.
Merrily, merrily shall I live now
Under the blossom that hangs on the bough.

Prospero: *Why, that's my dainty Ariel! I shall miss thee;*
But yet thou shalt have freedom: so, so, so.
To the King's ship, invisible as thou art:
There shalt thou find the mariners asleep
Under the hatches; the master and the boatswain
Being awake, enforce them to this place,
And presently, I prithee.

Ariel:. *I drink the air before me, and return*
Or ere your pulse twice beat.

Gonzago: *All torment, trouble, wonder and amazement*
Inhabits here: some heavenly power guide us
Out of this fearful country!

Prospero: *Behold, sir King,*
The wronged Duke of Milan, Prospero:
For more assurance that a living Prince
Does now speak to thee, I embrace thy body;
And to thee and thy company I bid
A hearty welcome.

Alonzo: *Whether thou be'st he or no,*
Or some enchanted trifle to abuse me,
As late I have been, I not know: thy pulse
Beats, as of flesh and blood; and, since I saw thee,
Th' affliction of my mind amends, with which,
I fear, a madness held me: this must crave –
And if this be at all – a most strange story.
Thy dukedom I resign, and do entreat
Thou pardon me my wrongs. – But how should Prospero
Be living and be here?

Prospero: *First, noble friend,*
Let me embrace thine age, whose honour cannot
Be measur'd or confin'd.

Gonzago: *Whether this be*
Or be not, I'll not swear.

Prospero: *You do yet taste*
Some subtleties o' the isle, that will not let you
Believe things certain. Welcome, my friends all!
        (V i 58-125)

– Activity –

Imagine you are the director of a production. Read these speeches carefully, thinking how you can make them come to dramatic life on the stage.

Copy the text above and paste it on to a larger piece of paper, keeping it to the left, with plenty of room on the right for your instructions. In one colour put all your suggestions to the actors – how certain lines should be delivered etc, and in another colour add all the suggestions to the stage manager about lighting effects, music, etc.

You will probably need to make a stage plan on which to plot your main moves, blocking in the action in general terms. You have only a small section of the play here, but you will need to allow for what led to it and what follows it: for instance, some inner stage seems to be needed for the discovery of Ferdinand and Miranda.

– Follow Up –

You may like to develop your production scheme with some drawings of the setting and of costumes. *The Tempest* is especially stimulating to a designer since it is not firmly placed in any historical period and has elements of a fairy tale. So your imagination could devise any costumes and setting you like: you could also incorporate some of the images or themes you find in the play – like the sea, or the Golden Age.

You can of course apply the same method to any other scene or fragment of the play. How would you stage the opening storm? What about the Masque? Work with a partner on any other section of the play you choose.

Another possible follow up is to get another group to present your scene, with you directing them.

Dramatic Conflict

– Evidence –

The Tempest is not mere spectacle or story of a magician's supernatural dominance of men and spirits. Nor does it lack suspense. The conflict that makes drama is present in Prospero, and its resolution comes, not so much of physical, as of moral and mental travail. ... Desire for vengeance has apparently lain dormant in Prospero through the years of his banishment, and now, with the sudden advent of his foes, the great wrong of twelve years before is stirringly present again, arousing the passions and stimulating the will to action.

– F Davidson, *The Tempest: An Interpretation*, 1962

There is no suspense in the play because Prospero can control future as well as present action. His foreknowledge enables him to control all that occurs within the confines of the play. ... Nor can we believe that Prospero has yet to bring his fury under the control of reason. If he really had to wait for Ariel to persuade him to mercy, would he have arranged the union of his daughter with Ferdinand? Prospero has already brought order to himself and his island before the play opens.

– Rose Zimbardo, *Form and Disorder in The Tempest*, 1963

These are two very conflicting views of *The Tempest*. Which comes nearer to your own? Do you find a lack of suspense? If you have seen the play in the theatre did the outcome seem clear from the start, or soon after? Was there genuine suspense of any kind? Look at these lines of Prospero's:

> *At this hour*
> *Lies at my mercy all my enemies.* (IV i 263-4)

Do you feel that Prospero at this stage really intends to exact revenge? Look too at the exchange with Ariel (V i 16-32). Is it Ariel who puts the idea of forgiveness into his mind, or did he intend this all along?

– Activity –

In the struggle with his enemies Prospero has shown himself to be so much in command that we never really doubt who will come out on top. We feel, perhaps, they are just puppets manipulated by his strings. (Yet Sebastian and Antonio seem to remain unmoved.) Conflict, if it is present in the play at all, must therefore lie within Prospero.

Work in pairs to search for any evidence in the play of his inner conflicts, or conflicts he has already resolved before the play begins. (See also the activity on *Prospero's Magic*.) Choose a team of about three people to be Prospero: the rest should question them about his inner feelings and conflicts. Any of them may answer. Use the evidence you collected to direct attention to specific moments and lines in the play.

– Follow Up –

Use the material to write an essay on the dramatic qualities of *The Tempest* in the theatre.

The Storm:
Group Presentation

– Procedure –

The opening scene of *The Tempest* is an excellent one for group performance and provides a stimulating introduction to study of the play.

The class needs to divide into two groups – about two thirds as the crew and one third as the court party. All the lines in the scene should be shared between these two groups, so that every person gets at least one line. Longer speeches can be divided into sense activities and shared by several people. It is a considerable saving of time to write these out on cards before you start.

Now transform the working space into some sort of ship, deciding on entrance points from cabins for court characters and allocating the crew to working parties – some to haul down sails, some to lower anchors, some to wrestle with the wheel, anything that might be going on in such a storm. Sound effects can help enormously; perhaps a few people could use cymbals and other percussion to swell the noise, and the human voice can be a very effective sound effect for wind and waves.

The whole scene should be a flurry of activity and noise, with orders shouted over the wind, and with constant and unwelcome interruptions from Alonso's party.

Give yourselves time to learn the lines by repeating them over and over again in different ways, then assemble in a circle to hear the lines in order and to learn cues. The first draft of the performance can now begin and the volume of the sound effects adjusted. The climax will need to be organised – some great crash of sound perhaps, with all the characters being thrown to the ground. Suggestions about how to improve the first attempt should be discussed, and several run-throughs will be needed before a definitive performance is achieved.

– Follow Up –

Make notes on the contrasts between the reactions of Court and crew.

Story In Stills

– Procedure –

It is important to understand that formalised symbolic tableaux are what is required rather than realistic presentation, so a good warm up activity is to work in pairs on statues and sculptors. Each in turn is sculptor and moulds the other into a symbolic shape to represent an abstract; start with more concrete ones like a sports person or dancer, but move quickly onto greed, hunger, pity, etc.

Alternatively, or additionally, work in threes on holiday postcards – a tableau from each group to represent a holiday destination in symbolic form, for the others to guess. Once tuned in to this way of working you will think much more imaginatively.

Working in groups of fours or fives, each group selects one of the following to present in a series of three freeze frames:

1. Sebastian and Antonio's plot against Alonso. (II i)

2. Stephano and Trinculo's meeting with Caliban (II ii) and the scene which follows.

3. The banquet presented and then snatched away (III iii), with Ariel's Harpy speech.

4. The "glistering apparel", IV i, line 165 to end of scene.

The sequences are then shown to other groups who guess what is being represented and discuss how successfully the underlying themes came through.

Example: *Here enters* Ariel *before: then* Alonso, *with a frantic gesture, attended by* Gonzalo; Sebastian *and* Antonio *in like manner, attended by* Adrian *and* Francisco: *they all enter the circle which* Prospero *had made, and there stand charm'd; which* Prospero *observing, speaks:*

This extract from V i will serve as a useful illustration before starting – perhaps the whole class could try this one as an example.

– Follow Up –

1. There is a natural step from this to dumbshow or mime – from frozen pictures to a stylised form of slow action. Any sequences from the play can be presented in this way, as long as you keep in mind the need to look at the essence and not the details of plot or storyline.

2. Another idea is to speed up movements like a silent film. The result will be comic but laughter is a great aid to memory.

Question and Answer:
A Teacher Directed Activity

– Procedure –

Students need to have a good knowledge of the play to do this and it can be useful for revision.

Select from the text a series of short questions and answers, enough for each student to have one or the other, and write each on a separate card. Then shuffle the cards and give one to each student. Students then go round the group repeating their phrase over and over until they find its partner. The only restriction is that they may not say anything other than the line on the card. When question and answer are reunited, the pair join a circle round the outside of the group and wait until everyone has completed the task. Ask each pair to deliver question and answer and tell the rest who they are and the circumstances of the exchange.

Examples

Dost thou forget From what a torment I did free thee?	No.
Hast thou not dropped from heaven?	Out o' the moon, I do assure thee.
What is your name?	Miranda. – O my father, I have broke your hest to say so.
Dost thou hear?	Your tale, sir, would cure deafness.
How shall this be compassed? Canst thou bring me to the party?	Yea, yea, my lord: I'll yield him thee, asleep.
Wherefore did they not That hour destroy us?	Well demanded, wench: my tale provokes that question.
But how should Prospero Be living and be here?	First, noble friend, et me embrace thine age, whose honour cannot Be measured or confined.
How now? moody? What is't thou canst demand?	My liberty.

– Follow Up –

Students can devise their own versions of this game. The lines do not have to be questions and answers; they could be any line and its response.

Another follow up activity is *Quotation Charades:*
Groups of about six have to guess the quotation which has been given to one of their number and which is conveyed to them by mime and gestures. Whoever guesses it then runs to the organiser for the next and repeats the process. The team completing all the quotations first is the winner.

Exchange of Insults:
A Teacher Directed Activity

– Procedure –

The idea behind this activity is to involve students directly in the language of the play and, at the same time, to explore a little of the antagonism between Prospero and Caliban.

Divide the class into two groups – Caliban and Prospero – and give one line of "insult" to each student. It doesn't matter that more than one should end up with the same insult. Perhaps you could photocopy the lines and cut them up to distribute. Now ask students to make the lines their own by walking around and repeating them in various different ways and with different expressions. When students are familiar with their own insults, line them up facing one another, Calibans opposite Prosperos. Start by getting each to shout his or her insult to the person opposite, who then responds. Then experiment with adding movement – the insulter advancing and the receiver backing away, perhaps, or a more elaborate pattern involving all students; they could weave in and out of the opposing group, delivering the abuse to a particular person, eyeball to eyeball. Ask the class to make suggestions on how to bring out the qualities of the language.

A group performance is the climax of the activity.

Examples

Caliban:

As wicked dew as e'er my mother brush'd
With raven's feather from unwholesome fen
Drop on you both!

A southwest blow on ye
And blister you all o'er.

All the charms
Of Sycorax, toads, beetles, bats, light on you!

You taught me language and my profit on't
Is, I know how to curse. The red plague rid you
For learning me your language.

Prospero:

For this, be sure, tonight thou shalt have cramps
Side-stitches that shall pen thy breath up;

                Urchins
Shall for that vast of night that they may work
All exercise on thee.

                   Thou shalt be pinch'd
As thick as honeycomb, each pinch more stinging
Than bees that made 'em.

Thou poisonous slave, got by the devil himself
Upon thy wicked dam

                      Thou most lying slave,
Whom stripes may move, not kindness.

               I'll rack thee with old cramps,
Fill all thy bones with aches, make thee roar,
That beasts shall tremble at thy din.

– Follow Up –

This activity will naturally lead to an exploration of the reasons for the exchanges. Ask the Calibans to search for lines which put his view – like

        This island's mine etc, (I ii 333)

and all the Prosperos to find their reasons in the form of quotations, for example:

               Thou didst seek to violate
The honour of my child. (I ii 349-350)

The exercise can then be repeated, with each student having one piece of evidence to deliver to the opposing side.

Hot Seat:
A Teacher Directed Activity

– Procedure –

This only works if the students know the play quite well, so it is ideal as revision.

Divide the class into groups of about five or six and allocate to each student a major character. Each group could contain: a Prospero, Caliban, Miranda, Ferdinand, Alonso and Antonio, or some similar combination. Each of these in turn takes the hot seat – a chair placed facing the half circle formed by the rest of the group, and, while occupying it, must answer in role the questions put by the rest of the group, who are not in character until their turn comes to take the hot seat themselves. The kinds of questions which work best are about motive or reactions to events; as much value lies in the framing of good questions as in the answers given.

You will find that there will be disagreements within the groups about some of the answers; these should send students back to the text for evidence.

– Examples –

- Prospero could be asked:
  "Did you always intend to forgive Alonso and your brother or was it Ariel's comment that made up your mind?"

- Antonio could be asked about his future behaviour and his possible repentance for the wrongs he did his brother.

- Miranda might be asked about her feelings towards her future father-in-law.

- It helps if the process is demonstrated to the whole class before they start, with the teacher participating either as occupant of the hot seat or as questioner.

– Follow Up –

A variation on this involves concentrating on one character, say Prospero, and having several students instead of one speaking for him and answering the questions put by the rest of the class.

Or the whole group can become Miranda or Caliban, to answer the teacher's questions in role.

All these techniques can lead to essay writing about the chosen character.

The BBC Video Version

(Note to the teacher: It is strongly recommended that Activity 8 [and perhaps an extension of it] be undertaken before the video is screened.)

Derek Jarman's 1979 film version being almost unobtainable, and Peter Greenaway's *Prospero's Books* (1991) too eccentric for classroom use, the BBC television version seems at the moment the only possibility. Fortunately, apart from a piece of technical ineptitude in the storm scene (where the studio wall, complete with framed prints, is clearly visible behind the sinking ship) this is one of the better examples of the very variable BBC series, with some impressive acting performances.

CAST

Prospero	–	Sir Michael Hordern
Miranda	–	Pippa Guard
Ferdinand	–	Christopher Guard
Ariel	–	David Dixon
Caliban	–	Warren Clarke
Gonzalo	–	John Nettleton
Antonio	–	Derek Godfrey
Alonso	–	David Waller
Sebastian	–	Alan Rowe
Stephano	–	Nigel Hawthorne
Trinculo	–	Andrew Sachs

Directed by John Gorrie

1. The great actor-managers of the early 20th century, like Sir Beerbohm Tree and Sir Frank Benson, chose to take the role of Caliban; the major actors of the second half of the century preferred Prospero. What do you think dictated these choices?

2. Sir John Gielgud played the role of Prospero in four stage productions, and was also Prospero in the film *Prospero's Books*. Each time his interpretation was different: a wise, humane Prospero, an irritable old man, a half-naked, biblical hermit, "an angry and embittered aristocrat speaking his thoughts as though they disgusted him" (*The London Times*, 1957). How would you describe Sir Michael Hordern's conception of Prospero? Does it match your view of the character?

3. The limited budget for the production made elaborate sets an impossibility. How well do the sets complement the action?

4. One of the advantages of film is that it can often handle magical elements more effectively than can stage productions. How well does the film make use of this advantage?

5. Ariel in this production is played by a young man, but the role - an extremely difficult one - is often taken by a woman. How effective do you find David Dixon in the role? Do you think the gender of the actor playing Ariel would make a difference?

6. Does Warren Clarke evoke sympathy for Caliban? Do you think his make-up is appropriate?

7. The play's epilogue is the actor's appeal to the audience for applause (a similar speech by Puck concludes *A Midsummer Night's Dream*) - asking release from his role by their clapping. Is it appropriate to have Prospero conclude the film in this way? In your group, devise another, primarily visual, ending.

Some Significant Stage Productions

(NB Much of the material in this unit is drawn from Christine Dymkowski's edition of *The Tempest*, which is referred to in the Preface.)

While many earlier productions of the play made Prospero a dignified, magisterial, noble figure, over the last fifty years he has been more often portrayed as a flawed human being. In one of earliest productions to offer a colonialist interpretation, Jonathan Miller's 1970 production at London's Mermaid Theatre, Prospero was, according to the *Daily Telegraph* and *The Times*, "a touchy neurotic, the victim of a power complex", "whose need for slaves [was] certainly as great as Caliban's need for a master".

How does this interpretation square with your interpretation of Prospero?

Miller's production emphasised the impact of colonialism on the New World by making both Caliban and Ariel black , and with a compliant Ariel and an antagonistic Caliban showing the two opposing ways in which native populations responded to the arrival of Europeans.

Sam Mendes' 1993 RSC production at Stratford with Alex McCowen as Prospero, Simon Russell Beale as Ariel and David Troughton as Caliban differed markedly from traditional interpretations in a number of ways. McCowen's Prospero was a more homely figure, taking up his ducal crown and blowing the dust off it; Simon Russell Beale is a brilliant actor, but one whose bulky physical appearance would seem to have disqualified him from the role. The in-the-round stage was bare except for three trunks or baskets. The play began with Ariel leaping out of one of the trunks and clapping his hands, whereupon a storm lantern descended and Ariel initiated the tempest "by setting the lamp swinging, his kohl-rimmed eyes following the wide arcs it [made] with the unnerving dispassion of a cat watching the twitches of a butterfly" (reviewer in the *Independent*). This was accompanied by thunder and lightning, and "quite suddenly...frantic figures [were] lurching this way and that". Prospero was dimly visible at the rear of the stage, seen through a blackcloth of clouds and sunset, "on a high-step-ladder watching over the pandemonium".

What does your group think of the idea of having Prospero visible as the storm rages about the ship?

Several other productions have shown Prospero actively controlling the tempest. In Neil Armfield's Australian production (1990) Prospero was shown whipping up the storm with his staff in a large drum of water.

Mendes' choice of Simon Russell Beale was so surprising that it inevitably focussed the audience's attention more than usually on the figure of Ariel, but characterisation as well as the appearance of the "tricksy spirit" was so unusual that some critics saw him rather than Prospero or Caliban as the central figure in the drama. Beale's Ariel barely concealed his hatred of Prospero, treating him, one critic remarked "with the barely concealed insolence of a head-waiter in a snooty restaurant"! This interpretation, of course, emphasised that Ariel was as much a slave as Caliban, and Beale made him into a dangerously subversive figure.

In your group discuss this interpretation. What evidence can you find in the text to support it? If you have seen the BBC video, consider how David Dixon's interpretation differs from Beale's.

In 1995 Neil Armfield restaged his 1990 production with a significant difference: he cast Kevin Smith, an Aboriginal actor, in the part of Caliban , and "to watch Smith [in loin cloth and tattered redcoat jacket] swagger around the stage like Jacky-Jacky, beaten, berated and plied with alcohol; to feel the power of his impotent anger at his dispossession; and to listen to him explain the music of his island to the drunken imperial clowns he has taken up with, is profoundly affecting" (*The Australian*).

A production in Birmingham in 1994 showed Caliban as white and Prospero, Ariel and Miranda as black. How do you think this would be interpreted by the audience?

Shakespeare on Stage: Drama Techniques

John Hughes, Senior Lecturer in Education, University of Sydney

This chapter draws attention to aspects of Shakespeare's plays as performed theatrical works. It will look beyond a mere analysis of the words in the script and will focus on those techniques relevant to the play as a staged performance.

In recent years emphasis has been placed on plays as performance pieces and for many students and teachers this has caused some difficulties. It is acknowledged that the field, especially the discipline of performance semiotics, is problematic for teachers and students alike:

> *Learning how to interpret and analyse theatrical events is a critical component in the education of students... However, there is very little available to guide teachers who are struggling...How are teachers supposed to help students become more responsive to theatrical events? What skills do students need in order to openly receive and actively interpret a variety of performance texts?* (Grady, 2000, p144).

This chapter provides guidelines for analysing a Shakespeare play as a live, theatrical event.

— Performance Semiotics —

Drama examination questions for senior students now demand an understanding of performance semiotics, that is, the signs which convey meaning from the stage to the audience, and the dynamic between the actors and the audience. Where once, in examination questions, there was a concentration on issues such as characters and themes, students are now faced with more complex areas to comment on.

For example in 2001 the following questions appeared in the English paper for the New South Wales Higher School Certificate:

2/3 Unit Common English, Paper II.
Question 3 (Drama):
In what ways do playwrights use dramatic techniques to present their ideas in the two plays you have studied from the list below?
Arthur Miller: *The Crucible*
William Shakespeare: *Macbeth*
Sophocles: *Antigone*
Katherine Thomson: *Diving for Pearls*.

English Advanced, Section II
Question 4:
How might different productions dramatise the struggle
between chaos and order in *King Lear*?

— Dramatic Techniques —

English teachers and their students are familiar with those elements of drama criticism which also apply to literary analysis. We refer here to the story, the structure of the work, characters, themes, motives, language, imagery, symbols, genre, socio-political context, historical context, gender issues and ideological positions. These areas are well covered when studying either a novel or a play. This chapter does not concentrate on these issues because most teachers and students are familiar with them. It needs to be stressed, however that the above aspects are also part of the dramatic devices of a play.

— Script and Performance —

One of the major developments in recent performance studies research is the way in which readers of scripts have begun to focus on the fact that play scripts are written to be performed and a critical response to a play must reflect the fact that the script is a blueprint for a live happening. The realisation of such an event will require the creative input of a range of talents. The performing arts involve enactments which bond audiences and performers in a shared set of experiences to which both make differing contributions; hence each performance of the same written text is unique (Hughes, J, 1998). The dynamics of actor and actor, actor and director, actor and audience, change with every enactment. It follows that students must study a play both in the theatre and as text, and that our study of text must all the time take account of what could be happening on stage. (Carlson, M, 1996)

However, there are students who write about a play, in examinations, as if the play were a novel. It is not uncommon to read papers in which students write "In the novel *Hamlet*, Shakespeare tells us about...". This confusion is not entirely unjustified because if one looks at the types of critical concerns teachers and students have traditionally applied to drama the following appear: themes, plot, character, structure, symbols, imagery and tone, and the like. In order to study a play as a performed work, students need to explore the fact that a play script is a springboard for collaborative action.

Unlike poetry or the novel, there is no intimate relationship implicit between the reader and a play script. A play script is written for a team – directors, designers, actors etc. – to bring to life. It is not possible to read a text for performance without responding to the different genre within the script. For example, at one point the reader will need to interpret as an actor, at another as a designer. Critical sensibilities and comprehension strategies must be developed which allow the reader 'to recognise that the play script consists of a set of instructions to actors, directors, designers and technicians' (Michaels, W, 1991).

This chapter looks at drama elements which particularly relate to plays as performance pieces. These are: plot, plot points, and plot and character, the theatre performance space, setting, lighting, focus, music and sound effects, props and costumes, actors, proxemics, pace and tempo changes.

— The Plot —

When reading a script, or seeing a play, it is important to draw a distinction between the sections of the plot that occur on stage and the story that we learn about. This is a useful distinction when exploring drama techniques because it draws our attention to the decisions a playwright has made concerning what will be highlighted on stage. Information that is presented though actions and words, on stage, is likely to have more impact on an audience's focus than information which is reported.

In terms of drama techniques, it is interesting to explore the parts of the plot Shakespeare decides will happen on stage and what we will simply be told about. For example, we learn, in *Othello*, that Othello and Desdemona are married. This is part of the story, but not part of the staged plot. The play is focussing on the events after Othello and Desdemona's marriage, not on their wedding per se. In *Antony and Cleopatra*, we do not see a coronation of Cleopatra because it's not central to the action of her relationship with Antony. We know she is Queen, that is part of the story, but how she got there is not a major part of the staged plot of *Antony and Cleopatra*.

— Plot Points —

A play, or any dramatic work of art, has a plot structure: the twists and turns that keep our interest and tell the story. Each point in the story, where the plot turns on its journey, can be called a **plot point**: the arrival of a character, the exposing of a secret, a discovery. The first plot point is when the audience realises what is at stake or what type of story this is going to be. For example, in *Romeo and Juliet* it is when the two teenagers meet. We already know the families are sworn enemies so a possible romance between the two teenagers signals the conflict and the drama ahead.

— Plot and Character —

The plot, in many of Shakespeare's plays, is often tied very closely to the actions of one or more characters. For example Macbeth plots his way to the throne; Romeo and Juliet have their separate plots that meet and destroy them both.

Teachers and students studying a Shakespeare play should fill out a basic play grid for each scene of the play in order to visualise what is happening on stage and follow the plot. The play grid should show: the setting, who enters, who exits and what happens.

— Theatre Performance Space —

The performance space is a major part of the dramatic techniques employed by a playwright. The space in which a play is performed conveys many drama messages. We have a very different expectation when we view a performance at an opera house from than we have when we view a performance by a travelling circus. When studying Shakespeare's plays, we have to envisage the Elizabethan performance space, such as the Globe Theatre, and what this would have meant for the audience.

The Globe was situated across the River Thames in the seediest part of town, amidst the other forms of 'low' entertainment such as brothels, bear baiting and cock fighting. People did not go along expecting a high- brow, cultured event (Gurr, A, 1987). They would wander in and out of the performances, eat and drink and have assignations. As a consequence, Shakespeare's plays have much repetition in them so that if you missed part of the plot the first time, you understood it the second time.

This is very different from the traditional theatre space that we are used to today. Now, the audience generally faces the stage, sits in the dark and fully concentrates on the play. Hence, in contemporary performances of Shakespeare's plays, much of the text is often deleted because we experience a very different theatre world, one where messages are sent and received in a more concentrated time and space frame.

— Viewing the Stage —

At the Globe Theatre, in Shakespeare's day, the audience sat or stood on three sides of the thrust stage. This meant that they interacted with each other and became part of the visual picture of the performance. The actors were performing to three sides and competing for the audience's attention. As the plays took place in daylight, the audience was as visible as were the actors. Some people could see very little of the performers. For instance,there was limited seating above the stage on the first balcony, known as the Lords' Boxes. Here the aristocracy or wealthy merchants would sit here so as to be seen by the masses.

— The Fictional Space of the Stage —

Unlike many of today's stages, the Globe used extremely limited set pieces, meaning that any indication of setting for scenes was conveyed principally through the language of the play. The fictional space of the performance changed rapidly and this is made plausible by the 'wipe and clear' method of staging, by which actors' entrances establish a new fictional space for each scene.

If the scene were to alter, for example in Othello, from a dark night street scene to a raging storm, the actors would have to establish this with the audience through their language. For example see how the scene is set in these words:

Act II, scene I

Montano: *What from the cape do you discern at sea?*

First Gent: *Nothing at all, it is a high-wrought flood.*
             I cannot 'twixt the heaven and the main
             Descry a sail.

Montano: *Methinks the wind hath spoke aloud at land;*
             A fuller blast ne'er shook our battlements.
             If it hath ruffianed so upon the sea,
             What ribs of oak, when mountains melt on them,
             Can hold the mortise? What shall we hear of this?

— The Stage Picture —

We know that Shakespeare did not write many explicit stage directions in his texts, yet settings, stage movements and actions are often embedded in the text (Styan, 1977).

— The Setting —

As we can see from above example from *Othello*, the setting in Shakespeare's plays is established by the words the actors speak; it is embedded in the text.

The setting is a major dramatic technique and conveys meaning. Indoor settings are often associated with more intimate relationships between the characters. For example, much of Macbeth is set indoors as the dark intrigues and murderous plots of *Macbeth* and Lady Macbeth unfold. These deeds eventually turn in upon themselves and destroy the Macbeths.

King Lear, on the other hand, is very much an outdoor play, and the huge themes encompassed in this play are reinforced by the wild elements to which its characters are exposed. As the personal tragedy of Lear unfolds and his alienation from those he loves becomes more extreme, the setting shifts increasingly towards the hostile, natural world. Note how the wildness of the setting is established in Lear's words:

King Lear, Act III, scene I

Lear:
> "Blow, winds, and crack your cheeks. Rage, blow.
> You cataracts and hurricanoes, spout
> Till you have drenched our steeples, drowned the cocks.
> You sulph'rous and thought executing fires,
> Vaunt-couriers to oak-cleaving thunderbolts,
> Singe my white head. And thou, all-shaking thunder,
> Strike flat the thick rotundity o' th' world,
> Crack Nature's moulds, all germains spill at once,
> That makes ingrateful man".

Kenneth Tynan, in his 1992 review of Peter Brooke's King Lear, wrote that the stage is "empty and sterile, a bare space of hostile earth".

You will find another well established and important setting in *Richard II* in Act III, scene iv.

Queen
> What sport shall we devise here in this garden,
> To drive away the heavy thought of care?

[First] Lady   Madam, we'll play at bowls.

Queen
> 'Twill make me think the world is full of rubs,
> And that my fortune runs against the bias.

[Second] Lady   Madam, we'll dance.

Queen
> My legs can keep no measure in delight
> When my poor heart no measure keeps in grief;
> Therefore no dancing, girl. Some other sport.

[First] Lady   Madam, we'll tell tales.

Queen   Of sorrow or of joy?

[First] Lady   Of Either, madam.

Queen
> Of neither, girl.
> For if of joy, being altogether wanting,
> It doth remember me the more of sorrow.
> Or if of grief, being altogether had,
> It adds more sorrow to my want of joy.
> For what I have I need not to repeat,
> And what I want it boots not to complain.

[Second] Lady   Madam, I'll sing.

Many critics see the garden as a significant metaphor for the themes in *Richard II*. Here we see another example of the setting forming part of the dramatic techniques of a Shakespeare play.

— Performances Today —

Nowadays a crucial factor in a performance of Shakespeare is that the setting can be established by scenery or in the cinema by the location. This can mean that the words used by Elizabethan actors to establish the setting verbally may be redundant in such performances.

— Stage Directions —

As noted above, Shakespeare did not write many explicit stage directions in his texts, yet, just as with settings, stage movements and actions are often embedded in the texts . In this section, we will looking at some of those embedded directions.

— Lighting —

Lighting can be used to evoke setting and mood and will change the appearance of a stage. In today's theatre the lighting will, for example, signify to us whether it is day or night. As we have already seen, Shakespeare's plays were performed in daylight and so if it is a night-time setting, the actor's words will need to tell us.

Macbeth is a very dark play and many of the scenes occur at night. For example, in Act 5 scene I, to establish the night setting for Lady Macbeth's sleep walking scene the Doctor says to the Gentlewomen:

> *'I have two nights watched with you...'*

and as Lady Macbeth enters he says:

> *'How came she by that light?'.*
> *So we know it is night!*

Shakespeare himself sends up this need in one of Bottom's speeches from *A Midsummer Night's Dream*. Bottom, as we know, is a very poor actor, but he wants to make sure that the members of Theseus' court, who are watching the play, know that it is taking place at night.

A Midsummer Night's Dream, Act IV, sc.ii.
Bottom (as Pyramus)

> *O grim-looked night, O night with hue so black,*
> *O night which ever art when day is not;*
> *O night, O night, alack, alack, alack.*

Lighting can also be used to draw focus to one space or character on stage. In Shakespeare's day, however, that dramatic device was not available, and so he would use other dramatic devices, such as movement, to draw focus to a character.

— Focus —

A skilled playwright can make sure that we focus on a particular character (or set of characters) in a scene so that we pay attention to their actions even though actions and words of other characters may be happening at the same time.

For example, in *Hamlet*, Act I, scene ii, there is a large cast on stage: Claudius, Gertrude, Councillors, Polonius, Laertes, Hamlet and many others, including Voltemand and Cornelius. And yet, our focus is on Hamlet. What is the dramatic technique that Shakespeare uses to make us focus on Hamlet? The court is very busy, with Claudius making large diplomatic speeches and various members of the Court making public speeches. Hamlet, we learn, is dressed in black and taking no part in the direct action except to make asides. He appears gloomy, and we learn this from Claudius' words:

> *"How is it that the clouds still hang on you?"*

In the midst of all this action, a character standing away from the action and juxtaposed to the action will still gain our focus even though he has little to say and moves very little. Shakespeare's isolation of Hamlet is a dramatic technique that focuses the audience on Hamlet.

An actor does not need to have lines to say in order to draw focus on stage. Another way to gain focus is for an actor to move. In Act V, scene ii of Hamlet, much is happening. Laertes and Hamlet are fighting and Claudius is seeking to hide his treachery. Look at the following exchange:

King Claudius *Part them, they are incensed.*

Hamlet   *Nay, come again.*

Osric   *Look to the Queen there, ho!*

Horatio   *They bleed on both sides.*
               How is 't, my lord?

Osric   *How is 't, Laertes?*

Laertes   *Why, as a woodcock to mine own springe, Osric.*
               I am justly killed with mine own treachery.

Hamlet   *How does the Queen?*

King Claudius *She swoons to see them bleed.*

We learn from these lines that the Queen has fainted. In the act of her falling down on stage, all focus would go to the Queen. This is a dramatic technique used by Shakespeare to draw attention to the Queen even though she has no lines to say at this point.

In today's theatre, focus is often given to a character by use of lighting. A spotlight on the Queen at this point in the play would also increase the audience's attention on her.

— Music and Sound —

Music can have several effects. It evokes mood, it can set the scene and often leads the audience to predict certain actions.

Music can be used before any text is spoken to set the scene. Ken Watson, the commissioning editor of St Clair Press, recalls a noteworthy production of *Twelfth Night* by the Royal Shakespeare Company where this was done. As the audience entered the theatre a group of musicians were playing tavern-like music. This changed to courtly music and then the Duke entered. He mimed courtly activities (reading submissions, sealing documents etc) with his courtiers. Only then when the scene was set did he say the opening lines.

Duke   *If music be the food of love, play on;*

— Songs and Dances —

There are many other examples of the use of music in Shakespeare's plays. Many of the plays feature songs and descriptions of dances. Characters often use songs to give insight into their emotional state at a given time, for example, Desdemona's "Willow song" in Othello. From Act IV, scene iii:

Desdemona   *My mother had a maid called Barbary.*
She was in love, and he she loved proved mad
And did forsake her. She had a song of willow.
An old thing 'twas, but it expressed her fortune,
And she died singing it. That song tonight
Will not go from my mind. I have much to do
But to go hang my head all at one side
And sing it, like poor Barbary. Prithee, dispatch.

Emilia   *Shall I go fetch your nightgown?*

Desdemona   *No. Unpin me here.*
This Lodovico is a proper man.

Emilia   *A very handsome man.*

Desdemona   *He speaks well.*

Emilia   *I know a lady in Venice would have walked*
barefoot to Palestine for a touch of his nether lip.

Desdemona   *"The poor soul sat sighing by a sycamore tree,*
Sing all a green willow.
Her hand on her bosom, her head on her knee,
The fresh streams ran by her and murmured her moans,
Sing willow, willow, willow.
Her salt tears fell from her and softened the stones,
Sing willow"-
Lay by these.-"willow, willow."
Prithee, hie thee. He'll come anon.
"Sing all a green willow must be my garland.
"Let nobody blame him, his scorn approve"-
Nay, that's not next. Hark, who is 't that knocks?

Emilia	*It's the wind.*

The song is a dramatic technique which displays Desdemona's feelings of desolation and sadness.

Songs can also be humorous, and act to provide a light-hearted break from the emotional gravity of surrounding scenes. This is well illustrated by the Gravediggers' song from Act V, scene i in Hamlet. The content is humorous but also underlines the tragedy of Ophelia's death and abandonment by Hamlet.

First Clown	*Cudgel thy brains no more about it, for your*
	dull ass will not mend his pace with beating; and when
	you are asked this question next, say "a grave-maker";
	the houses that he makes lasts till doomsday. Go, get
	thee to Johan. Fetch me a stoup of liquor.
	In youth when I did love, did love,
	Methought it was very sweet
	To contract-O-the time for-a-my behove,
	O methought there-a-was nothing-a-meet.
Hamlet	*Has this fellow no feeling of his business that a sings at grave-making?*
Horatio	*Custom hath made it in him a property of easiness.*
Hamlet	*'Tis e'en so; the hand of little employment hath the daintier sense.*
First Clown	*But age with his stealing steps*
	Hath caught me in his clutch,
	And hath shipped me intil the land,
	As if I had never been such.

There are also examples in the Shakespearian text where actors indicate that musical instruments such as trumpets were included in Elizabethan performances. These sounds often herald the entrance of significant characters. The following example is taken from *Richard II*, Act I, scene iii.

Lord Marshal	*My lord Aumerle, is Harry Hereford armed?*
Aumerle	*Yea, at all points, and longs to enter in.*
Lord Marshal	*The Duke of Norfolk, sprightfully and bold,*
	Stays but the summons of the appellant's trumpet.
Aumerle	*Why then, the champions are prepared, and stay*
	For nothing but his majesty's approach.

— Sound Effects —

We know that sound effects were also used in Elizabethan Theatre. There is evidence to suggest that barrels were rolled across the floor of the roof cavity above the stage to give the effect of thunder. An associated effect, the firing of a projectile, led to the destruction of the first Globe theatre in a performance of *Henry VIII* when the roof thatching caught fire and spread to the rest of the theatre.

— Props and Costumes —

Props and costumes are elements of the staged drama which, depending on their type, function and relationship to the space and actors' bodies, convey meaning to audiences (Pavis,1985: 209).

Props are anything that can be carried on stage; for example a sword, a candle, a goblet. They may or may not be used by characters, but are usually incorporated because they somehow change the workings of the play. For example, the handkerchief in *Othello*, the dagger in *Macbeth* and Ophelia's flowers in *Hamlet* are dramatic uses of props.

Props often become associated with a character and can be used to enhance that character when they are present or absent. For example, the wearing of a crown carries symbolic dramatic meaning, that is, the person is a king or queen.

— Costumes —

Costuming is an important aspect of live theatre performance. Costumes identify characters as belonging to social groups by providing such information as their social status, wealth and occupation. The colours and styles of costuming may also convey dramatic meaning by having symbolic significance. In Elizabethan times, a person's status and rank was determined by the costumes they wore. The Elizabethan costumes were elaborate, but familiar to Elizabethan audiences. They would know from the costume the status of a character as these social systems applied to themselves. Actors were considered scandalous as they dressed as royalty or as women.

— Actors —

When looking at dramatic techniques we cannot forget the casting of the actors and their style of performing (Pavis, 1985:210). The actors in Elizabethan performances were always male, with young pre-pubescent boys often playing the parts of women. This becomes especially significant when examining the way that audiences would have related to the tone of scenes. Whereas today's audiences would view scenes from *Romeo and Juliet* as romantic and weighty, perhaps Elizabethan audiences would have found the image of two men acting the part of male and female lovers hilarious.

Scenes in which Shakespeare describes the differences between men and women would also have been humorous to Elizabethan audiences given the cross-gendered casting that occurred. A good example is the Nurse's description of Romeo in Act II, scene v:

Nurse   *Well, you have made a simple choice. You know not how to choose a man.*

Romeo?   *No, not he; though his face be better than any man's, yet his leg excels all men's, and for a hand and a foot and a body, though*
they be not to be talked on, yet they are past compare.
He is not the flower of courtesy, but,
I'll warrant him, as gentle as a lamb. Go thy ways, wench. Serve God.
What, have you dined at home?

This is a very risque speech and, no doubt, the Elizabethan audience would have derived much humorous pleasure from it, especially as it is delivered by a male dressed up as a female.

— Actors' Status —

In Elizabethan days, actors were not considered as high-status professionals and often held other trades. In today's productions or films, the opposite is true. Consequently, today's audiences are far more likely to accept a relationship of separation between audience/actor than in Elizabethan performances. Familiarity, or lack of familiarity, with the real persona of an actor affects the way that audiences view a performance and place themselves within it.

In today's theatre and film, well-known actors come with what is called a tag. That is, the character traits developed from their previous performances. In the Mel Gibson film of Hamlet, we cannot completely divorce Hamlet from Mel Gibson's previous roles such as in Lethal Weapon. In terms of our reception of a performance, Hamlet played by Mel Gibson is a man of action. Kenneth Branagh's Hamlet does not carry this tag.

— Proxemics —

Vitally important... is everything to do with the performers' occupation of the space, their entrances, exits, other movements and gestures and the proxemic relationships that these moves and gestures set up between actors, spectators, objects and the space itself. These movements and the groupings become meaningful only when situated in the given space and they are the major means whereby that space is activated and itself made meaningful.
(McAuley, G, 2000: 8)

Shakespeare often uses spatial relationships between actors to create dramatic effects. If we look for example at the opening of Hamlet, we see Bernardo and Francisco moving quickly across the stage at midnight, setting the scene. Horatio and Marcellus enter and move about a lot, indicating that something strange is going on. The Ghost enters and is established as separate from the group. The stage proxemics establish a scene of tension and fear. We know that something perilous is happening.

Proxemics are often used to create great tension on stage. In 1989, the following question appeared in the New South Wales Higher School Certificate English examination paper:

Question 3: Read the following extract from Othello carefully.

What does the passage illustrate about the dramatic qualities and the concerns of the play?

Othello   *It is the cause, it is the cause, my soul.*
           Let me not name it to you, you chaste stars.
           It is the cause. Yet I'll not shed her blood,
           Nor scar that whiter skin of hers than snow,
           And smooth as monumental alabaster.
           Yet she must die, else she'll betray more men.
           Put out the light, and then put out the light.
           If I quench thee, thou flaming minister,
           I can again thy former light restore
           Should I repent me; but once put out thy light,
           Thou cunning'st pattern of excelling nature,
           I know not where is that Promethean heat
           That can thy light relume. When I have plucked thy rose
           I cannot give it vital growth again.
           It needs must wither. I'll smell thee on the tree.

           O balmy breath, that dost almost persuade
           Justice to break her sword! One more, one more.
           Be thus when thou art dead, and I will kill thee
           And love thee after. One more, and that's the last.

           So sweet was ne'er so fatal. I must weep,
           But they are cruel tears. This sorrow's heavenly,
           It strikes where it doth love. She wakes.

Desdemona *Who's there? Othello?*

Othello	*Ay, Desdemona.*
Desdemona	*Will you come to bed, my lord?*
Othello	*Have you prayed tonight, Desdemon?*
Desdemona	*Ay, my lord.*
Othello	*If you bethink yourself of any crime* *Unreconciled as yet to heaven and grace,* *Solicit for it straight.*
Desdemona	*Alack, my lord, what may you mean by that?*
Othello	*Well, do it, and be brief. I will walk by.* *I would not kill thy unpreparèd spirit.* *No, heavens forfend! I would not kill thy soul.*
Desdemona	*Talk you of killing?*
Othello	*Ay, I do.*
Desdemona	*Then heaven* *Have mercy on me.*
Othello	*Amen, with all my heart.*

This question, asking about dramatic qualities, caused many students and teachers great concerns as they didn't know what this meant. To answer this question, we need to visualise the stage picture. Desdemona is asleep in her bed downstage toward the audience. Othello enters from the back and slowly walks towards her from "It is the cause" to "I'll smell thee on the tree". Given the amount of words he has to speak here, it must be a very slow walk. When a character, that is intent on murder, moves very slowly to his victim, it creates almost unbearable tension in the viewer. We only have to think of those slow movements in Hitchcock, and other horror films, where tension and suspense is built by the slow movements of the camera. In answering this question on *Othello*, one of the key issues the students needed to note is the proxemic relationship between the two actors and how Othello's action of moving slowly toward Desdemona is a dramatic technique designed to charge the audience with anxiety.

— Pace and Tempo Changes —

A play is a performance piece. If we were studying music, it would be inconceivable not to analyse pace and tempo changes. In the great symphonies of Mozart and Beethoven, there are slow movements and quick movements (largo and allegro). Plays are also performance pieces and so good playwrights, such as Shakespeare, make sure there are tempo changes. A play that moves at exactly the same tempo throughout the entire performance becomes very monotonous and boring for an audience.

In Shakespeare, we often find slow movements followed by very fast movements and this is a dramatic device. The following examples give some idea as to how these changes in pace/tempo take place.

An example of this dramatic technique can be found in *Hamlet*, Act III, scene iii and Act III, scene iv. In Act III, scene iii, Hamlet has a long speech in which he contemplates killing Claudius.

Hamlet	*Now might I do it pat, now he is praying,*
	And now I'll do 't,
	and so he goes to heaven,
	And so am I revenged. That would be scanned.
	A villain kills my father, and for that
	I, his sole son, do this same villain send
	To heaven.
	O, this is hire and salary, not revenge!
	He took my father grossly, full of bread,
	With all his crimes broad blown, as flush as May;
	And how his audit stands, who knows save heaven?
	But in our circumstance and course of thought
	'Tis heavy with him. And am I then revenged
	To take him in the purging of his soul,
	When he is fit and seasoned for his passage?
	Number
	Up, sword, and know thou a more horrid hint.
	When he is drunk asleep, or in his rage,
	Or in th' incestuous pleasure of his bed,
	At gaming, swearing, or about some act|
	That has no relish of salvation in 't,
	Then trip him that his heels may kick at heaven,
	And that his soul may be as damned and black
	As hell whereto it goes. My mother stays.
	This physic but prolongs thy sickly days.

The tempo of this long speech juxtaposes with the tempo of the short, sharp lines that follow between Hamlet and his mother in the next scene:

Hamlet	*Now, mother, what's the matter?*
Queen	*Hamlet, thou hast thy father much offended.*
Hamlet	*Mother, you have my father much offended.*
Queen	*Come, come, you answer with an idle tongue.*
Hamlet	*Go, go, you question with a wicked tongue.*
Queen	*Why, how now, Hamlet?*

In order to change the tempo, Shakespeare will often juxtapose a very grave and grim scene with a humorous scene.

Macbeth, Act II, scene ii, is a very serious and intimate scene in which Macbeth and Lady Macbeth discuss the killing of Duncan. It is immediately followed by a riotous and robust scene by the Porter. This juxtaposition not only changes the pace but would give the groundlings entertainment.

In the concluding scenes of the *Macbeth*, Shakespeare builds the tension by placing a number of short but extremely active scenes together. These scenes depict the warring of Macbeth and Macduff's respective factions. By placing a series of short, fast scenes together where actors are walking on and off in a nearly continuous stream, Shakespeare builds the pace and tension. The pace and tension is interrupted by the scene in which Lady Macbeth's death is reported. These shifts in pace and tempo draw the audience into the action of the play and direct the audience's attention to various characters or occurrences.

When studying a Shakespearian play, one should look for Shakespeare's use of the dramatic technique of tempo and pace changes.

— Conclusion —

The great drama educator, Dorothy Heathcote (1979), stated that a theatrical performance consisted of only six basic elements:

Sound	Silence
Movement	Stillness
Lightness	Darkness

She challenged us to find anything more. It is arguable that there is more. However, she has highlighted that plays are living performance pieces and that we must analyse the dramatic techniques and activities that are happening on stage. As Grotowski, the famous twentieth century director stated "...the theatre is an act carried out **here** and **now** in the actors' organisms, in front of other men (sic)" (1969: 119).

When studying a Shakespeare text, we need to visualise the performance as taking place within a defined space. Further, we must visualise how an audience would be reacting and responding to this.

Drama techniques consist of the conventional aspects: characters, structure, themes, language, socio-political context etc. However, for a full understanding of drama techniques used in Shakespeare's plays we need to address the stage picture: theatre space, the theatre performance space, setting, lighting, focus, music and sound effects, props and costumes, actors, proxemics, pace and tempo changes.

Students should approach the study of a Shakespearian play as if they were going to direct a performance. They should ask themselves at all times the following questions:

- What is the performance space?

- What is the relationship between stage and audience?

- What is the setting?

- What time of day is it?

- Who enters?

- What do they say?

- What do they do?

- Who has the focus?

- Where are characters in relationship to others on stage?

- What are they wearing?

- What props do they use?

- What is the tempo of the scene?

- When do characters exit?

The answer to these questions, together with the more familiar literary criticism issues (language, themes etc), will develop an understanding of the drama techniques employed by the playwright.

References

Carlson, M, 1996, *Performance: a critical introduction*, London: Routledge.

Grady, S, 2000, 'Languages of the stage: a critical framework for analysing and creating performance' in H Nicolson, (ed), *Teaching Drama 11-18*, London: Continuum.

Grotowski, J, 1969, *Towards a Poor Theatre*, London: Methuen.

Gurr, Andrew, 1987, *Playgoing in Shakespeare's London*, Cambridge University Press.

Heathcote, Dorothy, 1979, *Three Looms Waiting*, (Video Cassette), BBC Omnibus.

Hughes, J, (1998), 'Teaching Plays As Theatre', In W Sawyer, K Watson and E Gold (eds), *Re-viewing English* (pp 277-285), Sydney: St Clair Press.

McAuley, Gay, 2000, *Space In Performance, Making Meaning In Theatre*, University of Michigan Press.

Michaels, W, 1991, 'Teaching Texts' in Hughes, J (ed), 1991 *Drama in Education: The State of the Art*, Education Drama Association New South Wales.

Pavis, Patrice, 1985, 'Theatre Analysis: Some Questions And A Questionaire' *New Theatre Quarterly*, Vol 1 (2) May, pp 208-212.

Styan, J L, 1977, *Shakespeare's Stagecraft*, Cambridge University Press.

Tynan, K, 1962, 'King Lear', Review. *The Observer*, November.